USEFUL
BELIEF

USEFUL BELIEF

**BECAUSE IT'S BETTER
THAN POSITIVE THINKING**

CHRIS HELDER

WILEY

First published in 2016 by John Wiley & Sons Australia, Ltd
42 McDougall St, Milton Qld 4064
Office also in Melbourne

This edition first published in 2020 by John Wiley & Sons Australia, Ltd

Typeset in Sabon LT Std 11/13 pt by Aptara, India

© Helder Consulting Pty Ltd 2016

The moral rights of the author have been asserted

ISBN: 978-0-730-38539-4

A catalogue record for this
book is available from the
National Library of Australia

Cover design by Wiley

Cover image © procurator/Getty Images, Inc.

Printed in Singapore by Markono Print Media Pte Ltd

10 9 8 7 6 5 4 3 2 1

Disclaimer
The material in this publication is of the nature of general comment only, and does
not represent professional advice. It is not intended to provide specifi c guidance for
particular circumstances and it should not be relied on as the basis for any decision
to take action or not take action on any matter which it covers. Readers should
obtain professional advice where appropriate, before making any such decision.
To the maximum extent permitted by law, the author and publisher disclaim all
responsibility and liability to any person, arising directly or indirectly from any
person taking or not taking action based on the information in this publication.

Contents

About the author

Chris Helder is one of the most exciting speakers on the public speaking circuit in the world right now. A dynamic presenter, his highly entertaining speeches on influence have transformed how businesses communicate with their clients.

Chris has wowed more than 2000 audiences throughout Australia, New Zealand, Asia, Europe and the United States. He is a frequent TV and radio guest who talks about the power of genuine communication.

Originally from the United States, Chris graduated from Colorado State University and served two years as part of the distinguished 'Teach for America' program, completing his teaching in Compton, California. A certified practitioner of Neuro linguistic Programming (NLP, INLPTA), Chris has synthesised his work from NLP, human typological analysis, advanced communications, motivational research and behavioural modelling.

Drawing from many different fields of research, Chris has created something simple yet powerful in his keynote talks. His combination of energy, wit, humour and tailored content ensures he relates to every audience member.

Chris Helder's previous titles include the bestseller *The Ultimate Book of Influence* (Wiley).

He lives in Melbourne, Australia, with his wife, Lucy, and their three boys, Jake, Billy and P.J.

Preface

I am a motivational speaker—but I really don't like that title. I think it labels me in a way that somehow makes me seem like I'm not a regular person, when the fact is I'm dealing with a lot of the same stuff that everyone else is.

From establishing an identity to building relationships, all of us are riding this thing called 'life'. We all have to deal with the obligations that come with all kinds of commitments in many different areas—financial, business, relationship, parenting, family, friends and health.

Over the past 14 years, I have presented to more than 2000 audiences. I have been a keynote speaker, trainer, facilitator, coach and mentor to hundreds of thousands of people. I have witnessed many people spend endless energy on trying to change things they have absolutely no control over. Even if they don't *want* to change things, they spend a phenomenal amount of time worrying about them.

My goal in writing this book is to give people a simple tool that will help them focus on what is truly 'useful' in making the most of their life.

I was at a Christmas party last year when a man (who seemed to have had a few drinks) approached me and said, 'I heard you are a motivational speaker.' He snickered. 'Why don't you say something to motivate me?'

I laughed and tried to brush it off, but he persisted. 'No, seriously, what do you tell people? Do you tell people to be positive? Is that what you say? "Be positive"?'

I hesitated. His tone was quite aggressive. For whatever reason, he was trying to provoke a response.

'No, I'm serious. What is your thing? Why do *you* get to talk to people?'

I looked at him and realised he genuinely wanted to know. I suppose what he really wanted to hear was if there was anything new or different he should know about.

'No,' I said. 'I don't tell people to be positive. In fact, positive thinking doesn't really work.'

He stopped for a beat. He hadn't expected that, and I could tell that I had his attention.

So I continued, 'Imagine if you'd just had the worst year of your life and someone came up to you and said, "Hey come on man, you've had a bad year. Don't worry about it! Be positive!" How would you respond?'

'I'd want to punch him in the face.'

'Exactly,' I laughed. 'You see, being positive doesn't really work. Instead, I teach something called Useful. It's an idea called Useful Belief.

'Here's an example of how it works,' I went on. 'If you've had the worst year of your life, you don't need me to tell you to be positive. Instead, I would say to you, "All right, you've had a really bad year. You are at ground zero. The question now is, what is the most useful thing for you to do that will take you from zero to one? What is a useful strategy that will lift you from one to three?" Being positive doesn't give you results. Useful gives you a strategy to get out of the hole and get to the next level.'

He looked at me thoughtfully through the haze of Christmas cheer. 'I like that. Useful. That's good.'

I smiled. It's always good to win over a cynic.

This is a book about Useful. It is based on some simple, practical tools that will give you the power and a strategy to cope with your reality.

I have written the first three chapters of the book in the form of a fable, because I believe this is an effective way to communicate the power of this message. It is an idea that can be applied by every reader. We all face our own reality: this idea offers you a useful strategy for dealing with your particular situation.

Through the tale of a business traveller and three significant encounters on his journey, this book takes you on a journey of your own—to self-awareness, and an improved approach to business and relationships. You'll learn how *useful* is better than *positive*, and you'll uncover the utility of your past, present and future challenges. If you have challenges right now, just deciding to 'be positive' will not fix them. Useful belief and strategy will. This book shows you how to frame your challenges to make them surmountable, and how to formulate an action plan to take you where you need to be.

In the final chapter I draw these ideas together and outline seven key areas in which useful belief can be transformed into useful action.

It is about empowering you and your belief systems.

Whether we are aware of it or not, we all create our own reality. We can write and rewrite our own story. It is amazing how many opportunities break through for us when we have a useful belief.

Chapter One
A useful past

I was waiting for my coffee. They had said they would call my name when it was ready. I was tempted to check my phone—not for anything in particular, but just because that's what I do. That's what we all do. Just stare at our phones. I might look at Facebook, check email, maybe Twitter. Just flick through stuff. Then they called my name.

'Simon?'

'Thank you.' I took the coffee. I had ordered a skinny latte—with two sugars, which obviously kills the 'skinny'. I'm not even sure why I ordered the latte, as the milk bloats me. I should've ordered a long black with no sugar. I would have felt better if I'd done that. The long black tastes terrible, though.

The truth is I was stressed. Random thoughts were spinning through my head. I had been grumpy and very anxious lately. I guess it had been a busy time, at work and in my life. I had been asked to fly from my home in Melbourne

A useful past

to present at our software conference in Barcelona. While I was happy to do it, that's a long way to go to make a presentation. Seemed like something I could have done from my computer. But it was our global conference, and I was pitching the results of the Australasian team—and, after all, it was Barcelona!

It was then that I heard a familiar voice behind me.

I turned around to see two women deeply immersed in conversation. It took me a moment to take in the scene and to recognise Sarah, whom I had gone to high school with many years ago.

'Well hello stranger!' she said when she noticed me. 'Simon, how are you? It's great to see you!'

'You too,' I replied. She was smiling. Her eyes struck me immediately. They always had. Bright. Blue. Awake. 'Sorry, I didn't mean to eavesdrop. I just heard a voice I knew. This is a definite blast from the past.'

'It is indeed! This is my friend Emily,' Sarah said, motioning to the woman opposite her. Emily smiled out of the corner of her mouth.

'Nice to meet you, Simon,' she responded quietly. She had a strikingly calm persona that actually made me feel quite frenetic in her presence.

'Simon Davies!' Sarah broke in to recapture centre stage. 'What are you doing with yourself? Obviously about to take a trip.'

'I'm going to Barcelona. Or Singapore then on to Barcelona. I've got this software conference thing. It should be good. I've never been there before—and it's summer in Barcelona, after all. It should be beautiful.'

'Do you have to go anywhere right now or would you like to join us?' Sarah smiled and Emily motioned for me to sit down.

Again I couldn't help noticing how blue Sarah's eyes were. I think I might have been staring. I was a little reluctant to sit down because I didn't want to intrude. I knew Sarah, but not well enough that I felt entitled to interrupt her conversation. Also I sort of like my time alone in the airline lounge. I look forward to enjoying the free food and wine and being there by myself for a while before

A useful past

my flight leaves. I wasn't sure that I needed to be dialed into a session with this emissary from my past, no matter how blue her eyes. But after a brief hesitation I sank into a seat next to Sarah and across from Emily.

'So tell me, Sarah,' I began, 'what are you doing with yourself these days?'

'I'm heading up a business in the health care industry. Emily is my new assistant and will be working on some projects with me. We were just getting to know each other.'

I smiled at Emily.

'We're off to Singapore for a conference. Our business works specifically in the nursing industry. We were just talking about how much nursing has changed over the past 20 years.'

'I'm sure it has. Seems it has all become a little less patient-centric than it used to be,' I said. 'My mother was a nurse for 40 years.'

'That's right, I remember that. By the way, Simon, I was really sorry to hear about your dad. I heard about his passing at our reunion last year. How is your mother going?'

'She's doing pretty well. It's been almost five years now.' Saying it aloud, I realised I was surprised by how much time had passed. 'It's strange, because in some ways it feels like he was here yesterday. Other times it seems like the memories are starting to fade. Anyway, my mother is doing really well, thank you for asking. She has her friends and her garden.'

'That's good, Simon. I'm glad she works in her garden. It's so important to have a hobby to keep you going in the tough times.'

I agreed, even as it hit me that I didn't really have a 'hobby' I was passionate about.

'What about love? Is there anyone special in your life?' she asked with a coy smile. Time was treating Sarah well.

'Wow, straight to the personal questions today, Sarah,' I said, considering trying to dodge that one. 'But no, nothing right now. I've been close a few times. How about you?'

'Yes, I have two boys and a girl. John and I have been married 15 years now. It's amazing how time flies,' Sarah answered. 'Emily and I were just talking about relationships, life and how sliding door moments can change everything.'

'I was telling her about how I met my husband, Paul,' Emily jumped in. 'He's English ... Sliding door moments are pretty crazy. I met Paul at this pub that my friends and I were not even going to go into. We decided to pop in for a quick drink, and there he was. We met, and now we've been married 12 years.'

'Congratulations,' I said. It sounds like both of you are doing well. It is amazing how things like that happen, Emily. A chance meeting and your world shifts. I really do believe that everything in life happens for a reason.'

As I said those words I realised I was just being polite. I don't even know why I said it, because that wasn't really what I believed. In fact, I've always made fun of people who say things like that. I guess I was just trying to be nice.

'We were talking about those kinds of moments,' Sarah continued her thought. 'And I was just sharing with Emily a new idea I've discovered. It's so important in life to work out the things you can control and the things you can't control.'

'Sure,' I agreed, wondering where she was going with this. Lately I'd been feeling like there was actually nothing in my life I could control.

'The idea of sorting out what you can and can't control is hugely important in our business because we have to deal with so much bureaucracy,' Sarah explained. 'But I recently came across an idea that is even better. It actually shifts how we look at each individual situation we are in so we can get the best results from it. This is something you would be able to use in your business too.'

'Okay,' I said. 'I'm always up for something new.'

'The idea is called *useful belief*.'

'Huh. What's that? Tell me about this useful belief.' I smiled encouragingly. I was now thinking I might have caught them well into their conversation. It was possible too that they were a glass of wine ahead of me.

'This idea is changing our approach to business. During the course of any one week, we are overloaded with meetings, emails and people trying to take up our valuable time. We all live in a world of information overload. We are bombarded every day — and a lot of it is negative, even a bit soul destroying. Useful belief has simply made me a whole lot more effective in the face of all this. It's an idea that challenges us to pick through all this information, filter out the noise and just focus on what is useful.'

'Okay,' I said, again wondering where this was leading. 'Give me an example of useful belief.'

'Really it's about focusing on what is helpful in dealing with a situation we can't change. For example, I believe this is the greatest time ever to work in the nursing industry. I don't know if that's *actually* true. But here's what makes it so powerful: because I *believe* now is the best time ever to be in nursing, it makes me better at my job — because I am living in the present and making decisions about right now. Unlike so many directors who are trying to make decisions based on their own experience 20 years ago.'

'So if you are going to work in your industry, you need to believe it's the best time in the history of nursing, whether or not it really is the best time?'

'Exactly. Truth is irrelevant. Because once I have a useful belief about the present, I will see the opportunities that we need to capitalise on right now.'

'That makes sense,' I admitted, reflecting that I had definitely not had a useful belief about my own career in the past couple of years.

'Let me give you another example,' Sarah went on. 'We were talking about families before. Obviously, a lot of people hang on to their past. You and I went to high school together. Odds are we both know people who still dwell on things that happened to them when they were 17 years old. I meet people all the time who are still obsessed by the behaviour of their parents during their childhood. So here is an example of a useful belief: we had the parents we were supposed to have. Do you think that's true?'

'I'm not sure whether I believe that,' I said. 'I mean, I'm not sure I've really thought about it like that. I wish it was true. I guess if I had the parents I was supposed to have I'm sure they would have been a lot richer.'

We all laughed.

'Here's the thing, though,' Sarah explained. 'It doesn't matter whether or not it's true. It's *useful* to believe it is. If you believe that, it is easier to make sense of what you learned from your parents and the importance they had on your life.'

'I'm hearing you, Sarah,' I said. 'But I'm just not totally sold on this idea of truth being so malleable. I mean, truth is truth, isn't it?'

'Simon, truth is often really overrated! And it usually doesn't help you get the result you want. What matters is whether or not that idea is a useful thing to believe. And truth is subjective anyway. If you and I went out to dinner, our interpretations of what happened at that dinner could be completely different. Maybe you thought it was the best meal you've ever had; maybe I hated everything I was served. Where is the truth in that? Most of the time what people believe to be true is really just their *perception* of reality. Therefore, we can all create our own reality.'

'Okay,' I said. 'Certainly there would be a difference between this reality and delusion. I can't just decide that I am a professional basketball player.'

'Of course not,' Sarah replied with a smile. 'But in the context of *all of our realities*, having useful beliefs is a game changer. Let me give you another example.

'We've all heard parents complain about the behaviour of "kids today". Like, "I can't understand these kids today and their computer games. When we were kids, we were outside playing. We were real kids. We had a stick and a ball and a bike! We stayed out until our parents flicked the porch light on and off, which was our cue to come inside for dinner. We were *real* kids!"

'This is not a useful belief. When people ask me I say, "I love this generation of kids. This is the greatest generation of kids *ever* in the history of the world! And it's the greatest time ever to be a parent!" If you ask me whether this is true, I'd say I don't care. I just know that believing it makes me a better parent.'

'Okay,' I responded, 'I think I agree with you. In fact, I think most people probably do this unconsciously on some level. They try to make the best of every situation.'

'That's close, yes…but it's not really it,' she said emphatically. 'The key is to ask yourself at a conscious level, "What is the most useful belief I could have about this situation I'm walking into?"'

By now Sarah had begun to pique my interest. It wasn't an entirely unfamiliar concept. I felt that most people talk about being positive in difficult situations. I had never put it together in such a simple yet powerful way, though. *Useful belief.*

'I have watched successful people over many years,' she continued. 'Do you know what I have noticed? They solve problems and keep moving forward. They deal with situations and they unconsciously ask themselves a simple question: "What is the most useful thing I could do right now? What strategy can I employ that would make this situation the best it can possibly be?" I want to help people bring this into their conscious awareness so they can use it in their everyday lives.

'How often do people go into a meeting believing it will be a complete waste of time? Mind you, it may not be a *great* meeting. But let's say you are required to attend. Once you know you have no choice about being there, ask yourself, "What is the most useful position I could take in this meeting?" This changes your entire approach to the meeting. Who knows? You might even get something out of it.'

Sarah shifted her body and squared up to me. 'In my business we go to conferences all the time. I have seen so many speakers over the years, and many of them say similar things. They say things like "Be positive!" or "When life gives you lemons, make lemonade!" These messages may make you feel good in the short term, but they are not really *useful*.'

I smiled. Having attended countless such conferences myself, I knew exactly what she was talking about.

'The reason they are not really useful is that sometimes life is *not* positive. Sometimes it's not lemonade! Sometimes things are just flat-out bad. You lose your job, your relationship ends, your father or some other loved one passes away. Positive thinking won't solve any of this. The question to ask is, what is the most useful strategy to move me out of this moment and into a better place? What can I believe that will help me out here?'

'I like it,' I acknowledged. 'It makes sense…I'm still curious about your comment about parents, though. You said we had the parents we were supposed to have. How can you know that? How is that useful?' The thought had never occurred to me. I know a lot of people who are successful *despite* their parents; there is no way they were the parents they were supposed to have.

'It's useful because it *is*,' she replied elliptically. 'They *were* your parents. There is no way to change it! Some people's biggest frustration is that they constantly try to change things over which they have no power. It is useful to believe that your parents were the parents you were supposed to have. They taught you about life—and often about who you do or do not want to be. Either way, the lessons were a gift you could handle. Not everyone could handle the pressure of having your parents. But *you* could. That's why they were *your* parents.

'It may be that none of what I just said is true, by the way. But you know what? It doesn't matter. Truth is overrated. Useful is simply more important than true when it comes to empowering yourself.'

'Nice,' I said as I took a final sip of my very average coffee. 'I like it. Even cynical me can see the value in that.'

'We were talking about this before you joined us. You have no control over who your parents are, or who your brothers and sisters are. You have no control over the city, suburb or town you grew up in. These are the cards you were dealt. But you have a choice in how you view those cards.

'Every day, people decide they have a reason to not be successful. Every person has a story they could tell as an excuse for them not doing their best. So, if that is the case, it is useful for that story to *mean* something, to have led us to where we are supposed to be. The idea that we all had the parents we were supposed to have is empowering. It means that it meant something, and that we learned something. It means our joy, happiness, suffering and pain were all supposed to happen—to teach us something.'

'Wow, you *do* make speeches,' I laughed. 'You always did, though. And you know what? I think you're right. I do not look at my life like this. In fact, lately I have been generally angry at the entire world. My beliefs haven't been very useful at all.'

'There's a question I like to ask my staff.' Sarah looked thoughtfully at me. 'I'll ask you the same question because I knew you back when you were 18 years old. If you could go back in time and give your 18-year-old self advice about life, what would you tell him?'

I stared back at her. How would I advise my 18-year-old self? Would I tell myself to do things differently? Probably. 'Look,' I said, 'I had a lot of things going on when I was 18. I made some mistakes. I'm sure most of us did. But there are definitely some things I did that were real mistakes. I regret them ... '

'I saw a TV interview one time, Simon. This female reporter was speaking with a man who had been a drug addict for a number of years. I was listening to his story, quite interested, as he told of how he pulled himself out of his situation. He went on to be hired for television, hosted his own show, and he was now being interviewed about his amazing story.'

I was listening, but then she said something that jolted me to another level.

'But the story wasn't what interested me,' she said. 'What interested me was the next question. Because the interviewer asked the very same thing I just asked you: "If you could go back and give your 18-year-old self advice, what would you say?"

'I remember thinking, what a stupid question to ask him! I mean the answer is obvious. He should tell himself, "Don't do drugs!" But what happened next got me thinking.

'The man looked at the interviewer and became a bit angry. He said, "I know what you're trying to do. You want me to look at my younger self and advise him to take another direction in life. Well, I want you to know something. I *wouldn't* do that. Every link in the chain has led me here—to being the person I am today. I did some horrible things to other people when I was on drugs. But you know what? It all led me to where I am today. And I am grateful for that."

'The next thing he said blew my mind,' she continued. 'He said, "I would walk right up to my 18-year-old self and say three words: *Just keep going.*"'

As Sarah finished her story, I flashed to myself at 18. Just keep going. I had so many regrets, and felt like I'd made so many mistakes. Could I walk up to myself at 18 and look myself in the eye and say, 'Just keep going'? If I did that, it would lead me right back to here.

A useful past

Then it hit me. Maybe *here* is where I am supposed to be.

'Well,' I said after a pause, making a move to stand up, 'this has been an amazing conversation. You have given me a lot to think about. I really like this idea.'

'I'm glad,' Sarah said. 'It was great to see you again.'

'It was really great to see you too, Sarah. Emily, very nice to meet you. I think there's a lot in our conversation for me. Anyway, I should probably put this useful idea to the test. What would be useful right now is for me to excuse myself as I am well behind in preparing for my meetings in Barcelona. So I'm going to go and do a little work, but I hope you have a fantastic trip to Singapore and wish you both all the best.'

Both of them smiled and shook my hand. I thought— okay, I wished—that maybe Bright Eyes would kiss me on the cheek. But she didn't. She shook my hand and we wished each other well. I was happy we'd caught up again and struck up a conversation. Useful belief. I got it.

I pulled my carry-on bag over my shoulder and made my way to a quiet table in the corner of the lounge. This conversation really had given me a lot to think about.

Here I was, a reasonably successful businessman off to Barcelona. Presenting at this global conference was quite a professional accomplishment. Despite this success, though, for some time I had been feeling a certain emptiness in my life.

I think I had been feeling a little disconnected ever since my father passed away, but I wasn't sure why. I know that since his death I had had a stronger sense of my own mortality. And I had developed a sense that nothing seemed really quite as important as it used to.

For one thing, I had become less emotional about the cycle of parents and children. While I still had memories of my father, I felt as though I was somehow losing control of them. As the years had passed, these memories had faded, the moments slipping into oblivion. Obviously, I was doing everything I could to hold on to as much as possible. But I couldn't help the fact that the gradual erosion of these memories and moments had left me feeling less significant somehow.

Losing someone close to you is a part of life, I reasoned. It is important to have a useful belief about it.

The conversation with Sarah brought back some strong memories. Recently these memories had hit me at the strangest times. I would be walking along the street and something would trigger an image of my dad.

I could still remember the phone call from my mother on the day he died. It felt as though I was a character in a movie. It was 6:30 in the morning and I was still a bit groggy as I picked up the receiver. Even through the fog I could sense the sadness at the other end of the phone.

'Simon, it's your mother here. I have some bad news. Your dad has died.'

It had been a call I had half anticipated. My father was 70 years old and had some serious health issues. He had just come home from surgery, but because the hospital had sent him home I had assumed he was going to be okay.

Some older people are ready to die. I don't think my father was. He was still working and in many ways seemed very happy. I think he had found a certain sense of peace in his life that had eluded him during my childhood. Maybe that's what made it so hard for me. It didn't seem 'useful' for him to die when he should have had so many great years ahead of him.

I tried to silence my thoughts. I had the long flight to Singapore ahead of me. I needed to just settle in and relax. That was a useful idea. Relax on the long trip to come.

Somehow, though, I just couldn't shut my mind off. I recognised that there were a lot of things in my life that weren't useful. I managed a lot of people in my job, and I felt like I flew off the handle all the time. I was stressed and actually a little angry. When push came to shove, a lot of things in my life were frustrating me.

This was brought into sharp focus when I boarded the plane to find the usual chaos of disorganised passengers blocking the aisle as they groped about in their bulging bags before trying to cram them into the overhead lockers—all seemingly in slow motion. What is *wrong* with these people, I thought, as I felt my frustration build.

Then, abruptly, I asked myself a simple question: Is it *useful* to get angry with a bunch of strangers you are about to share a long journey with? I smiled to myself. Probably not.

I was more than ready for them just to turn that seatbelt sign off and serve up the drinks. I've thought enough about useful stuff today, I decided.

A useful checklist

1 This is the best time in the history of the world to be in your industry/company/job. Is this true? It doesn't matter. It is useful to see the opportunities of the right now.

2 This is the greatest time ever to be a parent (and to be a child). When you believe this, you are more present as a parent.

3 This experience (meeting/trip/appointment/day) is definitely happening, so what is the most useful mindset for me to go into it with?

4 You had the parents you were supposed to have. True? It doesn't matter. It is useful to recognise that they taught you what you were supposed to learn, no matter how horrible or, for that matter, wonderful the experience.

5 The 'reality' of this situation is bad. What is the most useful strategy to lift me from ground zero to one? What is the most useful strategy to move me from point two to point five?

6 Everything that happens teaches us things.

Chapter Two
A useful present

Sitting next to me on the flight to Singapore was a well-groomed young businessman. He had a tailored suit and perfect hair, and I couldn't help thinking how successful he appeared for someone a decade younger than me. I took a look around the cabin for Sarah, but I could not see her. Part of me was slightly disappointed, but I decided that the most useful move might be just to settle in for some quiet time.

I watched a movie, which took me a couple of hours into the flight. I pulled out the travel book on Barcelona I had bought and began to make a plan of the sights I wanted to take in. There were many things I was excited about. Obviously there were the beaches, the tapas bars and the Spanish night-life to look forward to, as well as a stroll down the famous Las Ramblas boulevard to take in the heartbeat of Barcelona.

A useful present

I was particularly interested in the architecture of Antoni Gaudí. I wanted to see his famous La Sagrada Familia cathedral, still unfinished, even though the foundation was laid back in 1882. I was most excited about visiting Gaudí's modernist Park Güell. It fascinated me, mostly because it looked like a series of buildings out of a Dr Seuss book.

My excitement about visiting Barcelona for the first time was building. Not surprisingly, I hadn't given my speech much thought.

My immediate neighbour and I had yet to acknowledge each other. He would have been no more than 27, and he was clearly very busy. I had noticed out of the corner of my eye that he was poring over graphs, flow charts and other data, and emailing furiously. But since I was going to spend the next eight hours next to him, I decided to introduce myself.

'Hi, I'm Simon.'

'Hey,' he looked up from his screen. 'I'm Adrian.'

'You look like you're working pretty hard, Adrian. Do you have business in Singapore?'

'Umm, yeah...' Adrian glanced up again distractedly. I didn't think he really wanted to talk, which I realised I appreciated. I wasn't even sure why I had started the conversation with this golden child hotshot. I suppose I just wondered what he did. Anyway, I was happy to spend the rest of the trip in solitude.

'Sorry,' Adrian said a moment later. 'I just wanted to finish that thought and get the email off.'

'No, my fault,' I replied. 'I didn't mean to disturb you.'

'It's all good. I just had to get this presentation ready.'

'What are you presenting on?' I asked, only too aware that I had not finished my own preparation, and that instead I had just watched some silly romantic comedy.

'Actually, it's going to be a really interesting piece of business in Singapore. I'm doing a talk at a conference on how to influence the different generations in today's workforce.'

'That *does* sound interesting. What do you do that you get to talk about that?'

'I'm a generational expert,' he said. 'I know, that sounds like a weird title. But I have made a study of different

A useful present

generations, and my job is to share with people the keys to influencing the various generations of clients out there.'

'A generational expert ... ?'

'Yeah. I know, it probably sounds silly. But it's how I promote myself and they book me for these conferences, so it works for me.' He smiled sheepishly, a little embarrassed by his obvious self-promotion.

'Sounds good to me,' I said. 'But what exactly do you talk about?'

'It's very much about how to influence and interact with people of different age groups. It's sort of funny, but over the past few years there have been all of these speakers, trainers and authors who have tried to categorise my generation, Generation Y—that is, people born between 1981 and 1994. Basically, all they came up with was that we are really technologically savvy and better not upset us or we'll quit.'

I grinned at his joke. 'That sounds right to me,' I said. I saw his reaction and backtracked a little. 'You seem really busy, Adrian. You're obviously successful. But let's face it, your generation is a bit different, and that statement *does* seem to sum it up, in my experience. I've been frustrated with young people at work. I mean, they don't seem to take work as seriously as they should.'

Adrian sighed. 'A lot of managers feel that way. I try to challenge them in terms of their belief systems. My generation can tell if you don't respect them. I tell these managers that they need to have a *useful belief* about my generation.'

I stopped and stared at Adrian. 'What did you say?'

'A useful belief. I mean, if you want to influence our generation in the workplace, a useful belief is that we're all members of a really exciting, innovative, well-informed generation. If you are a manager of young people and have that belief system, my generation will want to work for you. That's because they want to be respected.'

Useful belief. Twice I had heard this concept, and in the span of only a few hours.

'Look at it like this,' he said. 'Let's say for a moment that you believe Generation Y is the greatest generation in the world. It doesn't matter if you think it's true. Truth can be a bit overrated!'

'That sounds familiar,' I said, starting to think the world had it in for me on this trip.

He smiled. 'If I am an older manager and I believe Generation Y is a great generation to manage, then guess what? I'm a better manager.

'You know,' he said, 'despite my age, I have had a chance to work with a lot of pretty successful people, and I've begun to figure something out. There is one fundamental thing that separates successful people from people who are average.'

'Okay,' I said. 'Hit me with it.'

'Successful people see opportunities that unsuccessful people don't see. I call it the Red Toyota Theory.'

'The Red Toyota Theory? Okay, with the day I'm having so far I'm looking forward to hearing this.'

'This is gold!' he laughed. 'Your brain has something called the reticular activating system, often referred to as the R.A.S. Successful people notice things other people don't because their R.A.S. is looking for these opportunities. But the great thing is that anyone can do this. For example, when you drove to the airport today, how many red Toyotas did you see?'

I thought about it. 'I don't remember seeing any.'

'Exactly! Your R.A.S. was not tuned in to spotting red Toyotas. However, if you made the decision to buy a red Toyota, you'd start to see red Toyotas everywhere. Your R.A.S. would be activated to search for them.

'It's no different with success,' he explained. 'When you set your R.A.S. to search for opportunities, then you start to see these opportunities everywhere. It's simply *useful* to believe that this is the greatest ever time to be alive. When you believe that, it is easier to practise gratitude and seize the day. Your brain will find beautiful things in the world because it is looking for evidence to support your belief. This is what makes it useful to believe this is the best year ever in your industry and your company. When you believe that, you start to see business opportunities everywhere.'

Hmm. I was starting to like this kid.

'Of course, the opposite is also true,' he continued. 'If you believe the markets are not going to let you make money, then you won't. If you believe the sales environment is terrible, you won't see ways to make sales. If you believe "kids today" are no good, you won't connect with your kids as well as you might. If you believe that managing Generation Y is awful and they're all lazy, you won't be able to connect with their way of looking at the world.'

'Wow,' I said. 'You and the universe are trying to tell me something today!'

He responded with a smile, though there was no way he could know what I meant.

'This is true of relationships too,' he went on. 'Your R.A.S. will sometimes torture you.'

'What do you mean?' I asked.

'Well, if someone has just broken up from a relationship that they really wanted to continue, the R.A.S. will torture them. They'll see happy couples everywhere. Couples holding hands, families having fun, children laughing and spending quality time with their parents.

'It also works the other way. If someone is unhappy in their current relationship, the R.A.S. will torture them too. What will they see? Hot singles, everywhere. Hot, single people who are unattainable!'

'That's hilarious, but I think you're right.'

'Well, I love the opportunity of working with people and helping them develop a clearer view of the different generations they work with,' he declared.

This guy was wise beyond his years, which was perhaps why I felt like I wanted to challenge him.

'You mentioned that by having a useful belief about the younger generation, you can do a better job managing them. Is there a way you teach people to influence and manage older generations as well?'

'Absolutely.'

I knew he was going to say that. 'So how would you influence *the older generation*? A lot of my clients are in senior management positions and have plenty of grey hair.'

'It's simple. Each generation is really easy to influence... Are you sure you want to hear about this?'

'Go ahead. We've got the time.'

He smiled. 'Okay, we'll start with the older people in the workplace and work back. Let's take the Baby Boomers first—the people born between 1946 and 1964, who are most likely to be at the top of the organisation. A lot of younger people from my generation are judgemental about older people in the office. They think the older staff don't understand them and don't have anything to teach them, so they ignore them and don't seek out their knowledge and wisdom. This, of course, is not useful.

'So what I teach them to do is to ask a very simple question of older people in the office. It's not the first question they ask, but I challenge them to find a time that is appropriate and ask them something that can change their relationship forever: "How did you get started in this business?" Instantly, you see the older person stop in their tracks as they size up this young whipper-snapper. "Well," they say, "It's an interesting story ... ", and they're off! At that point, my Generation Y colleagues have to do something that doesn't always come easily to them.'

'Listen!' I jumped in, smiling.

'Exactly,' he said. 'And not just listen — they also have to *care*. So I teach them some listening and caring techniques.

'No, I'm serious. Think about it. You were probably the same when you were young. You didn't want to listen to some older person tell you their story. You were probably pretty sure they couldn't relate to you. So I teach them affirmative responses like "Really?" and "Then what happened?"'

I laughed as his voice jumped up an octave with each response.

'I know, it sounds strange, but the higher pitch indicates that you care. Your voice goes up when you are interested. And it's not just listening and caring. I teach my generation to have a useful belief about the older generation. They have to understand their story. The oldest of this generation listened to the Beatles and Bob Dylan. They had Vietnam and the feminist and civil rights movements. They see themselves as a generation that had purpose.

'I mean, think about what this generation has lived through. They consider themselves the hardest working and most successful generation ever. If you doubt this, just ask them. They'll tell you!'

I laughed again. This was turning into an incredible day.

'I tell my generation to listen and to care, but also to look out for the moment when you know that you've won them over. See, so many people my age go out there with their cocky attitudes, trying to impress older people with their knowledge. But that's not going to do the trick. What will impress the Boomers is if you listen to *their* story. Eventually you'll realise that you've come to the moment when you've won them over. They look at you and begin to say something like, "Actually, this may be something you can use in your business..." And they offer you advice! Boom! That's the moment. When they start to give you advice, then you know you've won it.'

'Ha!' I said. 'That is gold! But I don't think that approach need be reserved for your generation's use. I think it's something I could use with the older people I work with.'

'Absolutely! It's in their DNA. Older people don't want to be *impressed*—they want to be *heard*. Let them give you advice; take that advice; and then, most importantly, *thank them* for the advice and they will love you for it!'

'That's awesome, mate,' I said. 'It seems like such a great idea. But...does it ever *not* work? Do you get any backlash when someone of your generation can't pull it off, you know, and have it seem sincere?'

'But it's not insincere. I'm teaching people to ask questions, to listen and care about what's being said. It's definitely not insincere. It's simply useful.'

'Useful. Love it. What about my generation? Generation X?'

'Your generation, those born between 1965 and 1980, is even easier to influence! You are the angry generation.'

I laughed out loud. He'd definitely got that right.

'It sounds a little harsh, but think about it: you were often the children of divorce, you tended to have fewer brothers and sisters, and both your parents worked. You spent a lot of time alone. More than that, though, you were the first generation that was expected to achieve in a time when you weren't sure what the rules were.'

'How do you mean?'

'You were the generation that was told you could— I mean *should*—have it all. Generation X women were taught that they should be corporate successes, domestic goddesses, *and* beautiful and sexy—all at the same time. Generation X men were also expected to become corporate powerhouses, but you were supposed to be sensitive new age men too. How could people have *any* idea what they were supposed to be?

'And Gen Xers weren't listening to the Beatles or Dylan. You were in a smoky bar with a beer in your hand, rocking back and forth to Nirvana or Pearl Jam. You were angry and confused. The music was called *grunge*, for God's sake. Before that you'd listened to punk and hard rock. You were angry.'

'You might be right. We had no lovefests like Woodstock, that's for sure.'

'Definitely not,' he agreed. 'You had something very different. You had AIDS! You had the Grim Reaper on television telling you that you might *die* from "free love".'

I snorted. 'You wouldn't have been alive when those commercials were on TV.'

'I was just born then. But anyone who has seen them knows what a huge impact they had on how you saw the world. Your generation was like the middle child. It was just harder for you. You began working, and got stuck in middle management. The Boomers have all the senior management positions sewn up and they are the healthiest sixty-somethings in history, which means they're not going anywhere anytime soon. You wanted the same houses they had, so you bought them. But your generation ended up with the highest mortgages and debt levels in history. You are also the greatest consumers of alcohol in recorded history.'

'Well, you are making me feel good now,' I said. 'We do have a lot going for us as well, though. I mean, it's a great time to be alive. That's useful, right?'

He laughed. 'Absolutely. I challenge Generation X to enjoy living in the moment. This generation crossed over from a simpler time into a frenzied world of technology. People of your generation are the last ones to remember not having a computer at home.'

'You're right. I didn't use a computer until high school.'

'Exactly. I challenge people to live in the now and experience life's moments as they come. Did you know that as a young child you would have laughed on average 300 times a day? That's because children live in the moment. They are not stressed about either yesterday or tomorrow. Adults laugh on average 17 times a day. Even more tragically, they are not embracing the moments. That's not useful.'

'All right, you may be right about some of that. Just out of curiosity, how do you teach people to "influence" us?'

'You mean, what is useful when speaking with Generation X?'

I grinned.

'Easy. It's actually the same question; it's just that the answer is different. I tell Generation Y to find an appropriate time in the conversation and then—when it feels right—ask, "So how did you get started in this business?" The question is the same, but the answer is totally different, and pretty hilarious.'

'What's the answer?' I hardly dared to ask.

He paused and looked up at me. 'They say, "Well, it wasn't easy! When I started in this business I had a cubicle, a phone and a phonebook. That's how I started." It's hysterical to listen as they begin to tell you their tough story. Again, I tell my generation to use all the listening skills we spoke about earlier. Listen and care. You Gen Xers love to tell the younger generation how tough you had it.'

I shook my head in defeat.

'Then I tell them that the end of the conversation also changes. Your generation is not going to give advice to a younger person. You're still battling through yourself.'

'What do you suggest, then?' I asked.

'Well, Generation X doesn't want to give us advice; they want to be affirmed. I teach the younger generation to look you in the eye and deliver a very simple line when you're finished with your story.'

'What is it?' This guy had me on the edge of my seat.

'It's simple. They look at you and say, "You've done so well. I really admire what you've done." Generation X walks away from the conversation and tells someone else, "Man I love those younger people. They appreciate what I've done to get here!" Gen Xers love affirmation — because they are in the middle of the war. They can't yet see the forest for the trees. They are stressed out working longer hours, raising kids, working their way up the ladder. They love it when young people appreciate the work they've done. I tell Gen Y to give them affirmation. It's just useful.'

'All right, hotshot,' I said. 'Don't ask me how I started in my business! I won't tell you.' I grinned at him. 'So what about Generation Y? What's my useful approach to your generation?'

'My generation is all about one circle.'

'What does that mean?'

'Well,' he explained, 'the Baby Boomers look at the world in terms of two circles. There is the professional and the personal. There are things you do at and for work, and things you do at home or out with your friends and family—and they believe that, for the most part, these circles should never cross. There is a way to behave professionally and, very possibly, a different way to behave personally. And these two worlds are kept separate.'

'Right,' I agreed.

'Your generation began to challenge that notion a bit. You are the first generation to cross those circles. Partly because you're so angry. You feel it's okay to do personal things on company time. For instance, you do your banking during work hours. If anyone asks you about it, your response will be defensive. "What do you expect? I'm working these longer hours for less return—when am I supposed to do my banking?!"'

He was clearly enjoying this. 'Okay,' I said. 'We are angry. I get it.'

'Yeah, but here's the point: Generation Y has one big circle and it's called LIFE! That's it. They say, "This is ME!" They are happy, mostly, for you to see their photos in social media because they're fine with the big circle. They can be at work, prospecting for new business, updating their status on social media, posting a photo and carrying on a conversation at the same time.

'If you are going to manage Generation Y, it's useful to embrace their view of the world. So here's a useful belief: *this is the most exciting, visual, well-informed, open, connected and energetic generation in the history of the world.* I challenge leaders *not* to get bogged down in whether or not that is true.

'It's simply useful to embrace the different generations. When you embrace the journey that the Boomers, Gen X and Gen Y have taken, you will simply be more influential, and they will want to work with you. So it's *useful.*'

What a day I was having! Two amazing conversations in the span of just a few hours. As Adrian and I finished up, I realised I needed to move around a little.

'Wow. Adrian, thank you,' I said. 'I've really enjoyed this conversation. You've given me a lot to think about. I think you might be right, too. I know I spend too much time worrying over problems and have too many expectations of others. I'm sure I need to open up a bit and think about what's going on from their perspective. This chat was most definitely useful for me. I know you'll be fantastic in Singapore. Now, if you'll excuse me, I'm going to stretch my legs a bit.'

'Good stuff, Simon. It's great to meet you,' he said, pulling on his soundproof headphones.

Part of me had wanted to keep the conversation going, but I'd heard enough. Parents. Business. Generations. What is useful? I really *did* have to go to the bathroom; but I also felt like my head was going to explode. Amazingly, the first two people I had met on my trip shared the same philosophy: useful belief. I imagined what it would be like if I faced every challenge by asking the simple question,

'What is the most useful thing I could do from here?' I definitely liked the idea.

I got up, stretched and looked around at my fellow passengers. Every one of them had worries, challenges, stress. Every single person was trying to deal with the challenges in their own life. Strangely, I had this overwhelming sensation of calm. The weight that I normally carried with me seemed to have temporarily lifted. I could see things in perspective. I had gained some clarity. For a moment, it all felt good.

We landed in Singapore and began filing out of the plane. I wished Adrian well for his conference. I felt incredibly lucky to have met him.

Somehow I still missed Sarah and Emily in the press of travellers. They'd probably headed off to baggage claim while I hurried to make my transfer. I was glad to have seen Sarah again. She too had given me much to think about.

The long haul from Singapore to Spain was uneventful, but I did spend a lot of time thinking about how bogged down I had become in my life. I was spending a lot of time worrying about things I couldn't control. I wasn't in a place where I was pushing myself to be better. Instead, I

A useful present

had become complacent. The more I thought about it, the more I realised that complacency led a person to focus on and be constantly frustrated by the little problems in life that *really don't matter*.

After some serious thought, I determined that it's actually pretty easy to be consumed with negativity, and to be drawn to the lowest common denominator, when you are not thinking in a way that is useful. It became clear to me that our society had become consumed by lowest-common-denominator thinking. Reality television dominates the airwaves. The nightly news is dominated by sensationalism. It is easy to get sucked into the vortex of negativity, celebrity and superficiality that modern society celebrates.

I wanted to think instead about empowerment. I wanted *power* — not the kind that leads others to feel resentful and jealous, but rather that inner power that would allow me to feel that everything would be okay. After all, that belief is useful. What was the alternative? That everything was *not* going to be okay?

I stepped off the plane in Spain feeling renewed. I was ready to embrace this conference. I was going to open myself up to new ideas and look on this trip to Barcelona as an adventure. After all, it had to be useful for me to be here.

A useful present

A useful checklist

1 This is the best time in the history of the world to be alive. That is useful!

2 This is the best time to be with my company and in my industry. It doesn't matter whether or not this is true — because it is useful. (Unless, of course, it isn't. In that case it's important to figure out what it is you want to do. You know what it is, and that it's the best time in history to try that thing!)

3 It's the best time in history to be a manager of young people. Generation Y is the greatest generation ever to manage. That's a useful belief if you are managing Generation Y.

4 Influence Baby Boomers by asking them to share their 'story', and listen to their advice.

5 Influence Generation X by understanding their 'tough story' and offer them affirmation on their journey.

6 Don't get frustrated. When you face challenges, ask yourself a simple question: 'What is the most useful strategy to move me forward from here?'

Chapter Three
A useful future

I checked into my hotel, which towered over a beautiful beach within walking distance of the sights and sounds of Barcelona. It was absolutely sensational—and, even better, my room overlooked a stretch of beach. I was awestruck. It was summertime, and the beach was packed with people. I quickly unpacked and left the hotel.

I came out on the beach, with towel, sunscreen and book in hand, and began to walk to settle into my little utopia. The day was hot, the sounds and sights fantastic. Families together, groups of young people hanging out, everywhere people kicking soccer balls or playing other games or diving into the waves.

I set down my towel and looked around, but immediately I knew I did not want to sit—I wanted to move. My mind was racing and I felt emotional. I strolled along the edge of the water for an hour before turning back.

I wanted to walk all of my anxiety out of my body. I felt like the more I walked, the closer I would be to getting this feeling *out*. Even though I was watching people around me, I felt invisible. Everyone on the beach seemed to be absorbed with the people they were with or the things they were doing. I suddenly felt very alone, which was odd, because I don't normally feel that way when I'm travelling. The sense of isolation was overwhelming. I felt like something was missing somehow. And it had to do with the future and the path I was heading down in life.

The conference was due to start the following day. I knew that in a matter of hours I would be surrounded by my peers and would no longer be alone. I didn't anticipate that seeing those people was going to help me, though. Somehow I was feeling like I needed some clarity about what I wanted to do with myself.

As my mind continued to race I found myself thinking about the past. Sarah had said that I had the past I was supposed to have. Was she right about that? It would surely be easier if that were not true, if I could blame my parents or other people from earlier years for my current emotional confusion.

And was Adrian right? Was this the best time to be alive? Well, just for a moment, as I looked around this golden beach in Barcelona, I thought that life couldn't get much better than this. I decided to focus on enjoying my walk, embracing the beauty around me and mentally preparing for the conference. Despite the long journey and thought-provoking conversations, I was ready for it.

* * *

The next morning I was soon engaged in small talk over coffee with my conference colleagues. While making my way into the main hall, I met Americans, Europeans, people from all over the world, many of whom had also made a long trek to be here in Barcelona. And in two days' time I was going to have my 15 minutes of fame.

The opening speaker didn't look that impressive at first glance. She was middle-aged and rather overweight. She hobbled up onto the stage in a flowing dress that hid her shape and began to speak slowly in a southern American accent. She was a writer and poet and had been quite a pioneer in her life.

What happened next shocked me. This woman gave a speech that provided me with the final piece of the puzzle that changed my life forever. That might sound pretty strong, but that's what she did. She spoke about the area of life in which I was most unsure of what I wanted. She spoke about the *future* and the power of having clarity about the future.

There was palpable anticipation in the air as this woman took the stage. I was certainly open to hearing what she had to say — more open than I'd been in a long time. Even as she started to speak, I had the sense that this was something that was going to be important for me to hear — something that would be *useful* for me.

Perhaps it was because her message spoke to me in such an unexpectedly personal way that I feel I can reproduce what she said that day fairly accurately. Maybe too it was how uncannily it jibed with and built on the two inspirational conversations I had had during my journey out. Of course I don't pretend to recall it all word for word but here, more or less, is the part I remember most vividly:

'Let's talk about the future. The great thing is that we can create a "perfect world scenario" into the future. I am going to share with you a tool that can help you *master your timeline* and gain great clarity about what it is you want to achieve over the next two months, the next six months, the next 12 months — or even the next 55 years. This is a tool for creating "hunger". The lack of hunger in people's lives comes directly from a lack of clarity about what they are hoping to achieve. As I often remind people, he or she who shoots at nothing generally hits it!

'Let me ask you a question. Have you ever felt like a day, a week or a month goes by, and the next thing you know six months have gone by, and you're not actually sure if you are even on target for what you want to achieve? Are you actually moving towards where it is you want to get to?

A useful future

'A lot of people try to set goals by living in the moment—and that's a problem. Many folks out there in the big wide world of life are living and working and surviving on what I call the "hamster wheel of life". That hamster is going round and round, working really hard, but is he moving in any specific direction? These people are the same. They get up every day, work hard, and run on and on inside that hamster wheel. At the end of the day, they're tired—but they are not actually making progress towards where they want to get to in their life. They aren't reaching the level of accomplishment they had hoped for. Often they aren't even sure they're running on the right hamster wheel.

'The problem is that they are just *reacting* to what's happening in the present.

'I'm going to take you time travelling into the future. You can do it right there from your seat. Imagine it's three months from now. Imagine you're calling a friend and you say, "I've never been happier in my job than I am right now. I've never been more connected to my business than I am right now." What would it take for you to say those words? What could have happened between now and then? What did you do? What did you put in place? The answer is the action you need to take.

'Let's go forward 12 months from now. For you to walk into this room a year from now and have the body you want to have, for you to feel better physically about how you look, about how you're connected to yourself—what did you need to do? What did you change? The answer is the action you need to take.

'Now travel two years into the future. Imagine you have just had the most successful two years of your entire business life. You walk in and say to me, "I feel better personally and professionally than I've ever felt." What changed for you? What did you put into place? The answer is the action you need to take.

'It's no different in the long term. Most people spend their lives spinning on that hamster wheel. Imagine you are 90 years old looking back on the events of your life. You're sitting in your favourite chair, sipping a cup of tea in front of an open fire and reflecting on everything that has happened. You want to look back and say to yourself, "I have loved my life. I've lived my life the way

I wanted to live it. I'm fulfilled." In order to reach that point and feel that way about your life, what did you do? What risks did you take? The answer is the action you need to take, starting now.

'The answers about what risks to take, when to act and what to change may lie in the future. But the fact is, too many people get to 90 years old and look back on their life with tremendous regret. It is not the mistakes or the things they did that they regret, but rather it is the things they did *not* do. For you to feel a sense of fulfilment instead of regret, what did you do? The answer is the action you need to take.

'I've always been fascinated by the idea of "sliding door" moments, and how life can totally change in one moment as a result of one seemingly unimportant decision or circumstance. Make a different choice and life would be altered forever.

'I chose to stand up for what I believed in at an early age. I made the decision to write about those beliefs. For that, I had a lot of critics. Some of my early writing was driven from anger. I have been asked if I regret any of my decisions in publishing those ideas. I do not. Every sliding door moment led me towards being here today. And this is where I am supposed to be today.

'Many people out there have made choices in their lives that they regret. These regrets often cause them to develop a chip on their shoulder. Everyone goes through this to some degree, but some people experience it much more acutely than others. It "suffocates" them, frustrating opportunities for future success and possibility. Other people have fewer regrets and don't hold on to feelings of guilt or insecurity as tightly as others.

'These regrets may have been around decisions about what to study, whom to marry, whether or not to have children, your choice of profession, moving away from family and friends...the list goes on and on. Many people will tell me those decisions were the best things they ever did! Others will describe these moments, the decisions and the circumstances in which they were made, with tremendous regret.

'Often those sliding door moments and the corresponding choices are not even ours to make. Everyone can tell you of situations in which they had no control or power. These are the things people said to you, the things they did to you—the people who decided not to love you or who left you by passing away.

'All of these moments, decisions and circumstances are critical in defining the emotional baggage each person carries around with them. The more time people play in the arena of past regrets, the harder it is for them to live in the now or gain clarity about the future. Instead, they live their lives focused on the past and events that they have no ability to change. It is virtually impossible to influence others until you are able to master your own timeline. To do that, these regrets need to be transformed into *opportunities for learning*.

'Whenever something significant happens in your life, ask yourself two simple questions:

Why did this happen?
What did I learn from it?

'It is amazing how answering these two questions can take any significant negative event in your life and turn it into a useful lesson. When asked these questions your brain can't help but search for a positive response as to why a certain event happened and what you learned from it.

'I challenge all of you to do this with each of the regrets you have due to moments, decisions and circumstances in your past. Ask yourself those two questions. Because it is an incredible thing when you feel the weight of past regrets lift off your shoulders, and instead of oppressing you they now make you stronger. That belief is simply useful.

'So many people live much of their lives in the negative past. Be very careful to use the past as a source of learning rather than getting sucked into the woulda, coulda, shoulda. When you turn the negative past into learning, it will no longer hold you back. Instead, it will serve as a guide to making better decisions living in the now and moving confidently towards the future.

'I have had the opportunity to meet so many amazing people. Often I meet someone who possesses a quality I like to think of as a calm presence. It just feels like they are so in control of being and acting in a way that is congruent with who they are as a person. They are truly present and comfortable in their own skin. They're really good at just being themselves.

'I have always wondered what separates that kind of person from the many people who seem self-conscious and anxious much of the time, and I think I've figured it out: *they know how to handle their timeline*. They have freed themselves from the past by turning regrets into significant learning. They are clear about the future and because they are so good with where they have been and where they are going, they are able to *be* in the moment. They can be really present without being anxious.

'Show me an anxious leader and I will show you an anxious team. Show me an anxious schoolteacher and I will show you an anxious classroom. Show me an anxious salesperson and I'll show you an anxious client. Show me an anxious world leader and I'll show you an anxious society. Anxiety repels.

'The truth is that our lives change. The things we did to be successful in the past may not be the things we need to do to be successful now or in the future. My mother, who has passed on, was a hero to me. I can remember the lessons she taught me and many experiences of our shared past. I cherish the hugs and the joy of looking up to see her watching me from the audience. I hold those memories close to my heart.

'Healing comes when we move forward. It is about using the lessons from the past to create a better future. It is also about our determination to be a better person ten years from now than we are today.

'It is no different in business. The reality is, here too the past is gone. That chapter is closed. For many people, the way they did business in years gone by may not work today. The approaches they used in the past may not generate business and customer loyalty the way they once did.

'But they have some options. They can look at their current situation and ask themselves what they want to do about it.

» Do they idealise the past and yearn for a return to how things used to be?

» Do they wallow around in their current situation and, rather than taking action to change, persist with practices that are no longer working effectively?

» Or do they *accept and embrace a new reality*. This is useful.

'You can create your own new reality. The challenge of the journey is exciting. It is not about being infallible, but rather the opposite. I challenge you to embrace a new useful belief for your business. What are the things you need to put into action? Let's imagine that it's 12 months from now. You walk up to me at a conference and say, "This has been the best year of my life — professionally, physically and in terms of my relationship. I have never been happier than I am today." In order to bring about this change, what did you start doing? What did you stop doing? What did you keep doing?

'I challenge you to spend some time on this. Discover what your future is really all about. For you to be the person you really want to be, what new behaviours do you need to put in place? What new habits do you need to adopt? Pay attention to the patterns of language you use when speaking about the past. There is nothing wrong with remembering the "good times" and analysing past behaviour patterns. But it's more important that you jump with both feet into a *useful reality*.

'What is going to work today? What do you need to get rid of from your past? Tell your story in a way that gives you power. Make yourself the hero of your own story.'

———————

She walked off the stage to thunderous applause. I had heard it over and over again. Useful belief. There is a useful belief about my past. There is a useful belief about the world today. There is also a useful belief about the future.

I had never been so excited about mapping my future and working out the actions I needed to take. I felt a level of clarity I had rarely experienced in my life. In fact, I don't believe I had *ever* felt this way. I wanted to focus on one idea around useful belief:

I can create my own reality.

For too long I had let others dictate how I should fit into the box they had created for me. I needed to come up with a series of useful beliefs for *me*, to guide me.

I decided to walk away from the conference for the rest of the morning. I wasn't sure why, but after hearing that talk I felt like being alone for a while. As interesting as the global financial update was likely to be, I decided I needed a walk in the park. And not just any park, but the famous Park Güell.

I don't know much about architecture really, but reading up on Barcelona I had become very excited about seeing the creations of the Catalan architect Antoni Gaudí. There are examples of Gaudí's work throughout the city, but I did not really appreciate the scope of it until I climbed out of my taxi and entered the Park Güell.

The park contains amazing structures and buildings that in reality, close up, seemed even more like Dr Seuss illustrations than they had in the guidebook. The buildings are fascinating and the tiling simply unbelievable. Strolling through the park, it hit me that this park was the perfect experience to round out my journey. Antoni Gaudí *created his own reality*. His work was utterly different from anything I'd ever seen ... and it was wonderful!

I watched tourists and families moving around the buildings and pleasure gardens, past vibrant street entertainers and musicians. I was simply excited to be alive. What a useful feeling this was! It felt like the Red Toyota Theory was in overdrive and I was seeing opportunities and beauty everywhere.

What do I want my life to look like in 12 months' time or two years' time? How do I want to look back at my life when I'm old? What would I regret never taking action on?

I sat in the park and began to write it all down. Surrounded by the inspiration of Antoni Gaudí, I was inspired to create my future. It was time for me to gain clarity about what my time on earth was going to look like. As I sat amidst the music, and the celebration of this artistic visionary, I felt as though I was perfectly placed to reach for and use my own vision and creativity.

It was indeed a wonderful time to be alive. And that belief was most certainly useful.

A useful checklist

1 Create a 'perfect world scenario' for the next 12 months, two years and 55 years.

2 For you to feel great about each of those time frames, what would need to happen? The answer is the action that you need to take, starting now.

3 Identify the past regrets that hold you back and turn them into learning. Why do you think this thing happened? What did you learn from it?

4 Everything happened for a reason; everything led you to being here today. This is exactly where you are supposed to be.

5 Create your own reality and make yourself the hero of your story.

Chapter Four
From useful belief
to useful action

It really is a fantastic time to be alive. When we start to believe this, we start to see things differently.

What I like most about the idea of useful belief is how simple it is to apply it. Merely being conscious and aware of what is useful means your brain will seek out evidence to support you. The reticular activating system we discussed in chapter 2 will filter all the information you receive and present to you what is really important—and most relevant and helpful to your current situation.

I wrote this book as a story because I felt this approach would make the ideas easier to grasp and act upon. Simon is everyman. Like many of us, he is a little cynical, frustrated, angry and confused about his life. We can relate to him and see how simple changes could shift his life completely. I wanted to show that people do not usually need to completely reinvent themselves. For most of us, it may simply require that we open up just a little. I talk about a

3 per cent shift. It is about waking up to what it is you want to focus on.

Often people believe they need to make radical changes, to completely transform themselves. Of course, when they think like this, making any change at all becomes a major project. This tends to overwhelm them, which of course means they end up doing nothing and taking no action towards improving their life.

But a change this big usually isn't required. Adopting some simple useful beliefs to improve the results in your business and your life can have a significant impact. In this final chapter I'll share some of these beliefs, as well as some simple actions that will help your useful beliefs come to life.

These useful beliefs, featured in the figure and in the pages that follow, can be broken down to:

1   Time Management

2   Coding Success

3   Body Language

4   Being Present

5   Gratitude

6   Energy

7   Taking Action

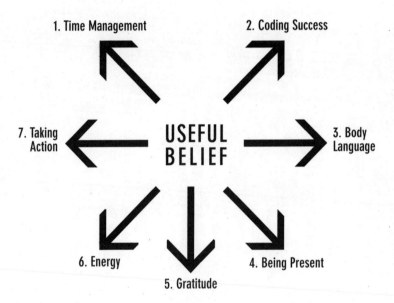

From useful belief to useful action

I can't do everything. I have to focus on what is most useful.

1. Time management

One of the biggest changes in modern society in recent years is the incredible amount of information we are assaulted with every day. This means it's never been more important to identify which information is going to be useful and to filter out what's just going to waste our time.

An essential means of dealing with this information overload is time management. I see so many people get sucked into activities that seem urgent, but are not really producing income or bringing in measurable results. In chapter 1, Sarah talked about how useful belief had allowed her to become much more effective in her job. She was able to avoid being diverted or sucked in by all the 'bureaucracy' and to focus on what was really important.

To ensure your time is used most effectively and productively, you need to ask yourself three questions:

- » What activities are most useful to the success of my role?
- » How long should I spend on these useful activities, and at what time of day?
- » What activities appear to be producing results but are not really having an impact?

Organisations send out reams of information every single day, a great deal of which will simply not be looked at by enough people to justify the time and resources used to put it together. Many people spend an incredible amount of time writing newsletters and other communications that will never be read. That is not to say that writing electronic newsletters, blogging and employing social media are not useful activities. However, it's critical to ask yourself a simple question: 'What is the *most* useful activity I can do today?'

Often, brand-building activities are more fun and less stressful than the income-producing activities. So people spend days on research, writing, database building, spending excessive time on social media and in meetings, none of which may produce direct results for their business.

For example, I present almost every day to a different organisation, which means I have very limited time left over in my week. So I am very conscious of how I allocate that remaining time. I can't do everything. I ask myself, 'What is a useful way of spending that time?' If it is useful, I do it. If it's not, I don't.

From useful belief to useful action

'Acting as if' will deliver a quick result.

2. Coding success

If you want to start implementing a change in how people perceive you, great news: you can start immediately! It begins when you deploy three simple but powerful words. As I look back on it, these three words fundamentally changed the course of my life. The words are *act as if*.

To be the person you really want to be, ask yourself: 'How would that person act in this situation?' Then act as if you are that person. Do the things they would do—and notice how quickly change starts to take place in our own life.

Say it is your ambition to be a great leader. How would you dress? How would you speak? How would you walk? How would you carry yourself? What would you think about? What things would you not bother to cloud your mind with? What books would you read? What sort of television shows would you watch, or not watch? What would be useful?

From useful belief to useful action

Adrian, whom we met in chapter 2, demonstrated many of the characteristics of success through the assured confidence with which he delivered his message. How was he dressed? How did he speak? How knowledgeable did he seem to be? One of the characteristics of success is simply making sure you know your subject. There is no substitute for competence.

Act as if you are, and change will start to take place immediately. You can have absolute clarity about what characteristics you would like to have and begin to act accordingly.

At the same time, it is very useful to code the success of others. In most industries and organisations, there are people who demonstrate clearly what success looks like. Whether it is the style and performance of the top salesperson or the training habits of the top athlete, it is usually very clear what these individuals do to achieve their level of success.

Starting a new job or joining a new organisation can feel quite uncomfortable at first. Fitting in can take time. So who does a brand-new member of the team spend time with? Typically, it is other new people! So the new people sit in the corner talking about the future and what they should do in their jobs to be successful. Of course, none has much idea what to do, and they're generally still unclear about what activities will lead to true success.

I challenge people to ask themselves a very simple question. Whether you are in marketing, sales, client acquisition, team building or any other area of business, ask yourself, 'Who in my company is best at doing that?' Once you know who that is, simply code the actions and behaviours of that person and begin replicating those actions. It is really very simple.

So when you join any new team or company or group, find out who represents best practice, introduce yourself to them and let them know you are new to the team. Tell them you recognise they are probably the best and that you will be watching them closely. If they have any advice to give you, you will be wide open to receiving their insights. Find out what they do. Code their attitude, activities and behaviours, and replicate them.

From useful belief to useful action

The 'mind-body loop' will change the perception people have of me.

3. Body language

The mind-body loop is alive and well. Healthy people have better posture than sick people, or sad people. Successful people have better posture than people who feel they are failing.

In the course of his journey, Simon's posture changed. As he was enlightened about new ideas he became lighter on his feet. He felt a weight being lifted from him.

If you watch someone with excellent posture, you'll notice that their body language conveys that they are alert and awake. Make no mistake, the mind follows suit. When the body is alert and awake, the mind is alert and awake too.

From useful belief to useful action

There is a way that successful people hold themselves. In meetings and conferences you can identify the best leaders by their distinctive posture. Carry yourself in a way that demonstrates that you intend to be successful! I see so many people sitting at the weekly meeting slumped over as though they can barely hold themselves up.

How do you present yourself in company and sales meetings? How do you sit at training sessions? How do you walk into the office first thing each morning? How do you carry yourself when you walk through the front door at home at the end of a hard day? What about when you are about to go to the gym or a workout? What posture do you assume when your children want your attention and want to show you something?

Other people in your life will respond to the physical posture you adopt when you approach them. So consider whether the body language you're using in your approach to others is useful. Not only can this improve your interactions with other people, but it will change your personal mindset through the mind-body loop. What the mind harbours, the body manifests. So be sure you adopt useful body language.

From useful belief to useful action

A useful belief will allow you to be present in the moment.

4. Being present

Do you believe that the eyes are the windows to the soul?

Eyes can be pretty amazing. I can be standing on stage and catch the eye of someone in the audience and immediately feel the intensity with which they are listening. I can feel that they are engaged in what I'm saying. Eyes create an instant connection.

Simon was attracted by Sarah's eyes. Sarah was very confident and her eye contact demonstrated this, as did the fact that she was extremely *present* in the conversations with both Simon and Emily.

Being present is one of the key benefits of useful belief.

Let's use the example of the meeting you have no choice but to attend. If you believe it is a waste of time, then your reticular activating system will begin to search for all the

From useful belief to useful action

reasons that confirm it is an unnecessary, unprofitable meeting. People do this every day. As soon as something comes up that covers old ground or is not results oriented, they see it: 'See, I told you. This meeting is a complete waste of time.' Approached with this mindset, any value in the meeting is likely to be missed.

On the other hand, let's say you walk into that meeting you can't avoid with a different attitude. You decide to adopt a useful belief about the meeting. You are confident that something productive will come of it, or that you will learn something or encounter some new ideas. Notice what happens then. Your reticular activating system will search for something useful to come out of the meeting. Maybe something useful will be there, maybe it won't. Either way, if it is there, you will find it.

Useful belief isn't just something we can incorporate in our professional lives. It comes into play in our personal lives as well. I have had two recent interactions with my children that illustrate this.

One morning my 15-year-old woke up and announced that he didn't want to go to school that day. He explained that he had been working hard (which he had) and he really needed a day off.

This was not going to happen. I explained it to him simply. 'Jake, you have to understand something. There is no possibility, and I mean *zero* possibility, that you are not going to school today. You are getting on that tram, going down Cotham Road and walking into that school. That is the reality of what is going to happen. That being the case, the only question is whether or not you are going to have a useful belief about today. If you do, you'll find opportunities to learn will be everywhere you look at school today. It's up to you what you do with that.'

Jake glowered and turned away from me, muttering, 'Stupid useful belief.'

I laughed at his response, but I know the idea has registered with him. That afternoon, when I asked about his day at school, he looked at me and said, 'I had a really good day. I thought about what you said.'

From useful belief to useful action

We all have our own reality and things we have to do. Part of Jake's reality is to go to school each day. I have to get on a lot of airplanes as part of mine. In the last financial year I gave 177 presentations around Australia, which meant 117 flights that year. That is the reality for me in order that I can do what I love to do. If that is my reality, it is important that I have a useful belief about it. What is my useful belief?

I love airplanes!

I love airport lounges. I love airline food. I love hotels. I love hotel sheets. I love travelling solo. I am alone much of the time. If you spend a lot of time alone, you need to get good at aloneness. Aloneness is awesome.

That is my reality. You have your reality. Develop a useful belief about it.

My second family example had to do with my 10-year-old playing a football game. P.J. and I arrived at the field in torrential, freezing rain. I said to him, 'We are definitely playing. We are going out there. If we believe we don't like playing in the wet and cold, we are going to be miserable. Let's get a useful belief going about this game. It's really fun to play in extreme wet and cold! Let's get as muddy as possible today!'

When you have a useful belief, you are able to be present and to enjoy the moment.

So often people focus their thoughts on other time frames. Sometimes that means being so focused on the completion of a goal that they fail to be present in the now and enjoy the task at hand. Other times it can mean being so focused on 'the way things used to be done around here' that they are unable to deliver or even understand how things need to be done today.

It is amazing how many parents are not present for their children. The child walks into the room and says, 'Dad, look at the picture I drew.' The father, who is busy in the kitchen, never really makes eye contact with his daughter. Instead, he glances fleetingly in her direction and responds

From useful belief to useful action

with a distracted 'That's great, sweetie, but right now I've got to get dinner ready.'

He didn't really look at the picture—or his daughter. Which means he missed an opportunity to connect with his child. To squat down beside her, look her in the eyes and say, 'That's beautiful, that is fantastic.' He missed the moment.

It's the same in almost any relationship. People get busy, they forget to focus on and make eye contact with the people they love. Your partner walks in and says, 'Hey, honey! How was your day?' You smile while checking your email on your phone and reply, 'Good ... good. Let me just do this quickly and I'll be with you.'

It happens all the time. When you fail even to make eye contact, you are not really present. Making eye contact and being present are useful actions, a product of having a useful belief about whatever activity you are doing.

How present are you? How good are you at looking at people directly and making the kind of eye contact that lets them know you are really listening to them and not distracted by other activities? Being present is very useful in the art of influence.

From useful belief to useful action

Practising gratitude changes my trajectory.

5. Gratitude

Do you spend most of your time appreciating what you have or obsessing over the things you don't have? Do you spend enough time focusing on the things and people you love—or do you brood over what's missing? Ultimately, do you spend most of your time thinking about the things that are 'right'—or worrying about the things that are 'wrong'?

It's very clear to readers that Simon had become cynical. His reticular activating system was no longer finding the beauty in the world. Even though it had been almost five years since his father's death, he remained angry at the world. Personal tragedy will affect everyone at some point in their life. A period of grief is natural and appropriate, but after some time it is important to adopt a more useful

From useful belief to useful action

approach by practising gratitude for the great experiences we have had.

I want you to wake up tomorrow morning and do the following exercise. Thinking about yourself, what are the first seven things that come to mind? The most important words are the words you say about yourself when you are by yourself. So what are those first seven thoughts? What do they focus on? Are they negative or positive?

For me, this is really about determining whether things are getting better or getting worse. We can all feel it when we are creating momentum in our lives and getting closer to what we want—or when we are not making progress.

One of my favourite words and concepts is *trajectory*. Every day has a trajectory. Is our day gaining steam or is it fizzling out? I am a huge believer in the idea that gratitude drives the trajectory of our day. In other words, when we start the day from a place of gratitude it is much easier to gain momentum towards creating success. Look back and determine what the trajectory of your life has been over the past 12 months. Are you more or less connected to your job than you were 12 months ago? Is your trajectory generally going up or is it going down?

Is your body, and general health and fitness, stronger or weaker than it was 12 months ago? Is your relationship stronger or weaker than it was 12 months ago? What is the trajectory of your life in these areas? Are they improving—or deteriorating?

Gratitude creates upward trajectory. Begin your day from a place of gratitude. The most important words you say all day are the words you tell yourself about yourself when you are alone. When those words are positive, you create a positive trajectory to build on throughout the day.

When you are grateful, the quality of your day improves. Creating a quality day is definitely useful, and gratitude will help your reticular activating system find the opportunities that exist everywhere around you. If you are cynical, you won't see even those opportunities that are right in front of you.

From useful belief to useful action

Energy is a decision.

6. Energy

Among all the successful people I have had the privilege of meeting and working with, I have never met a truly successful person who did not possess abundant *energy*. And this energy is contagious. But it's not a gift reserved for them alone. They have made the decision to possess and enjoy boundless energy.

Notice how important that last sentence is: *they made a decision to possess and enjoy energy*. Most people believe their energy level controls them, instead of the other way around. You are totally and completely in control of the level you have on any given day.

Energy is a decision. I want you to remember that statement, because it is one of the absolute keys to influencing others. You can't do it without energy. But the

From useful belief to useful action

good thing is you can draw on as much energy as you want. You just have to decide to have more. It is already present for you in abundance.

The fact is, most people choose to be tired. If you doubt this, then walk up to almost anyone on any given day, ask them and they will tell you. Often their response is pretty direct. 'Oh man, I'm tired today.' Ask them why. 'I don't know! I got 10 hours of sleep last night … I'm just exhausted.' Walk up to a young person and ask them. 'Yeah [yawn], I'm tired for sure.' Ask them why. 'I don't know. I'm 25 and have got my whole life ahead of me, but I'm wasted.'

It seems to be something many people have learned to say. I don't actually believe most of them are genuinely tired. Rather, it indicates a state of *disconnect*. They feel exhausted because they're no longer connected to their lives, their jobs and their relationships.

Energy is a decision. Because when you do feel connected to your life, you don't feel tired—you feel energised. Energy is one of those things you discover you have more of when you decide to be completely connected to your life.

Take the energy that is there for you. You can have as much as you want. And it's not possible to maximise your level of success and influence without it. Energy is a decision—and a most useful belief.

From useful belief to useful action

The butterflies are a gift from your body.

7. Taking action

I've discussed a lot of useful beliefs and actions in this book. But there's one thing that will stop people putting them all into action—and that is fear.

This fear is perfectly normal. It usually first manifests itself as a flutter of anxiety in the pit of your stomach. To be clear, I am not talking about the seriously debilitating anxiety some people suffer from, which requires more specialised attention. I am talking about the common 'flutter' we all experience, for example when taking action that may be outside our comfort zone.

This is a feeling that shows up in countless different scenarios. Everyone has procrastinated over something they should be doing. Maybe it's a phone call they need to make, a meeting they need to attend, a business opportunity they

From useful belief to useful action

should have followed up on, or even something as simple as paying a bill. We've all been through it.

The emotion that follows is guilt. We feel guilty for not making the call, or not doing the paperwork we should have, or not going to the gym as we promised ourselves we would. It's expected that people who feel guilty will become apologetic, but in reality their natural inclination is to move into a defensive, negative state. This is not useful.

What if we could change this? What if we could turn this anxiety into something positive and life-changing?

We can.

From now on, I want you to change the way you think about what this feeling signals. That flutter in your stomach is actually a gift from your body.

It is a signal to action — your body's way of getting your attention and encouraging you to do something. And it is completely positive. This, by the way, is a very useful belief.

Imagine if you changed your perception of that experience to something positive instead of negative? People commonly associate the feeling with words like 'anxiety' and 'fear'. These have incredibly negative connotations.

What if you changed the words? What if the flutter in your stomach was not fear or anxiety, but something beautiful? What if it was 'butterflies'?

The butterflies are a messenger. They are here to help you. They are your inner voice seeking to steer you in the right direction, calling you to do something. The butterflies are urging you to take action in a positive way to make your work and life better.

Remember: the most important words you say all day are the words you say to yourself about yourself when you are by yourself. Imagine if the words you say to yourself when your body sends you this message are: 'I NEED to do this.' And therefore you take action.

People avoid tasks they should be prioritising all the time. When I was at college in the United States, I had a friend who drove a big Chevrolet Malibu. It was a huge car and great for driving around a bunch of college kids. We had a lot of fun in that car.

One day I got in and saw that the oil light was illuminated on the dashboard. I said to my friend, 'Your oil light is on. Let's go put some oil in.' He declined and said he would fix it up himself.

From useful belief to useful action

The next time I got in his car, the light was still on. Again I offered to help him top up the oil. Again he put me off while assuring me that he would do it later.

A few days later I hopped in his front seat again—to find a business card wedged over the oil light. I asked him about it. He said, 'I know, but I got sick of looking at that oil light!'

The older I get, the more I like this story. My friend was procrastinating over something that was staring him in the face every day. It seemed ridiculous. Then again, most people do it. They know what they need to change their lives. Their 'oil light' stares them in the face every day. They know exactly what they should start doing or stop doing. It's right there in front of them. Most people, though, just hide their oil light under a business card and pretend it's not there.

I challenge you to identify the activities in your life that you should do more of and then to take action to get those tasks done. Be aware of what your body is telling you. In the past, you probably interpreted that shaky feeling in the pit of your stomach only negatively.

I challenge you to flip that. Welcome the butterflies when they come to visit you. Listen to their message and take action on a priority you have been deferring. Completing that task not only will give you a sense of achievement, but will give you a sense of control over your business and your life.

Hello, butterflies, thanks for coming to see me today!

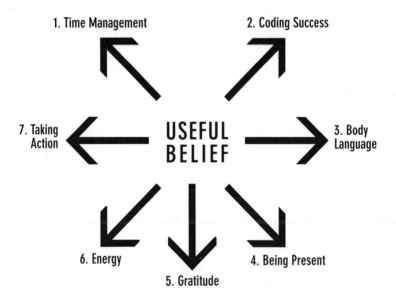

1. Time Management

2. Coding Success

7. Taking Action

USEFUL BELIEF

3. Body Language

6. Energy

5. Gratitude

4. Being Present

From useful belief to useful action

Useful final thoughts

I hope you have enjoyed this book. I have deliberately presented the ideas in a simple, accessible form. I wanted this to be a small book people could pick up and read on one flight—a quick experience, but one that left a lasting impression.

I have received so much feedback from people at conferences who have connected with the idea of useful belief. People have drawn links with religious belief, meditation, yoga, athletics, music, surfing and many other activities and ideas.

There is a lot of power in this idea. Some people have even shared their concern that it could be exploited to justify bad behaviour: 'I thought it was useful at the time.' The one caveat I would emphasise is that I don't believe *anything* is useful if the practice of it hurts anyone else.

Common sense is the key. (It usually is, by the way.)

We all have the moment at birth when we enter this world alone, and in the end we all leave it the same way—alone.

Useful belief is ultimately about how you choose to spend your journey in between. My goal is to help people be good to themselves on this journey. It is useful to be your own greatest friend. You will make mistakes—everyone does. That does not mean you have to beat yourself up about it for the rest of your life. After all, that wouldn't be useful.

We live in a time of unprecedented self-absorption and self-indulgent behaviour. Who would have thought only a few years ago that we would happily broadcast our life (or our version of it) on social media for the world to inspect? As Adrian suggested, we live in a world where increasingly there is only one circle—and that circle is called life.

My hope is that we can learn to better appreciate each other on our journey. It is useful to be happy for other people. It is useful to have people with whom to celebrate our victories and who can help lift us up after our defeats. Useful belief is ultimately about believing in ourselves. It is about believing that our journey matters. That it is important.

Be good to yourself.

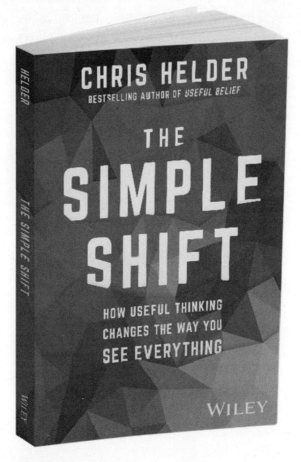

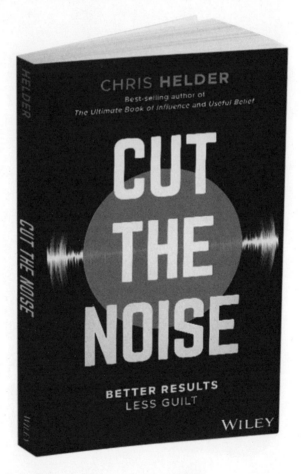